★ IT'S MY STATE! ★

West Virginia

Rick Petreycik

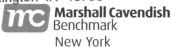 **Marshall Cavendish**
Benchmark
New York

Marshall Cavendish Benchmark
99 White Plains Road
Tarrytown, New York 10591-9001
www.marshallcavendish.us

Library of Congress Cataloging-in-Publication Data

Petreycik, Rick.
West Virginia / by Rick Petreycik.
p. cm. -- (It's my state!)
Summary: "Surveys the history, geography, economy, and people of West Virginia"--Provided by publisher.
Includes bibliographical references and index.
ISBN-13: 978-0-7614-2216-7
ISBN-10: 0-7614-2216-1
1. West Virginia--Juvenile literature. I. Title. II. Series.

F241.3.P47 2007
975.4--dc22

2006037703

Photo research by Candlepants Incorporated

Cover photograph: Comstock Select / Corbis

Back cover illustration: The license plate shows West Virginia's postal abbreviation followed by its year of statehood.

The photographs in this book are used by permission and through the courtesy of: Corbis: 39, 42, 50 (top), 50 (bottom), 51 (bottom); Bettmann, 22, 36, 38, 51 (top), 51 (middle), 53; Richard T. Nowitz, 12, 19; H. David Seawell, 14, 73 (bottom); Charles E. Rotkin, 17; Wally McNamee, 18; Visuals Unlimited, 20, (top); Hans Reinhard/zefa, 20 (middle); Kevin Schafer, 21 (top); Stefano Amantini, 21 (middle); Medford Historical Society, 34; Neal Preston, 50 (middle); Joseph Sohm/Visions of America, 69; Lester Lefkowitz, 72 (middle); David Muench, 73 (middle); Carol Havens, 73 (bottom). Photo Researchers, Inc.: Scott Camazine, 4 (top), 4 (bottom); Steve Maslowski, 4 (middle), 20 (bottom); Leonard Lee Rue III, 5 (top); Anthony Mercieca, 5 (middle); Scott-Berthoule, 5 (bottom); Ken Foster, 21 (bottom); Kaj R. Svensson 72 (top); Paul Whitehill, 72 (bottom). SuperStock: 8; Michael P. Gadomski, 9, 47; Gene Ahrens, 12; age fotostock, 16; James Lemass, 44, 62. The Image Works: Andre Jenny, 11, 48; Topham, 24; Jenny Hager, 43, 64; Jeff Greenberg, 49, 55, 67, 71; Joe Sohm, 59. North Wind Pictures: 28, 29, 32, 33. AP Images: 45 (top), 45 (bottom); Skip Rowland, 54; Craig Cunningham, 66. Envision: Steven Needham, 68. West Virginia Department of Tourism, 10, 52, 56, 57, 74.

Book design by Anahid Hamparian

Printed in Malaysia

1 3 5 6 4 2

Contents

A Quick Look at West Virginia

Nickname: The Mountain State

Population: 1,816,856 (2005 estimate)

Statehood: June 20, 1863

Tree: Sugar Maple

The tall sugar maple, which sometimes reaches a height of 80 feet, is valued for its beauty, its hard wood, and its sweet sap. Every fall, many visitors come to West Virginia to view the sugar maples' magnificently colored foliage. The trees' lumber is used to make sturdy furniture and musical instruments, such as guitars and pianos. Maple syrup comes from the sap of these maple trees.

Bird: Cardinal

The male cardinal is bright red with a black throat. The female is a sandy brown and black, and has patches of red on its wings, tail, and crest. The cardinal became the official bird of West Virginia on March 7, 1949.

Flower:
Rhododendron maximum or Great Laurel

This type of rhododendron is sometimes called the great laurel or the big laurel. The rhododendron shrub has dark green leaves and clusters of white or pink blossoms. The rhododendron grows best in mountain foothills, such as those found in West Virginia. It became the official state flower in 1903.

4

Animal: Black Bear

This medium-sized bear usually has black or dark brown fur. Black bears have rounded ears, very small eyes, and five strong claws on each paw. They also have a strong sense of smell that helps them find food. West Virginia's black bears live mostly in the eastern mountain region. They like to eat nuts, berries, fruits, acorns, and roots.

Butterfly: Monarch Butterfly

The monarch butterfly has dark orange-colored wings with black lines and a black border speckled with white dots. When the insect is in its caterpillar stage, it feeds on milkweed plants. After it changes into the winged butterfly, the monarch sips nectar from plants. The monarch was named the state butterfly in 1995.

Fish: Brook Trout

One of the reasons why the brook trout was chosen as the state fish was because this type of fish is the only trout species—or type—native to West Virginia. Brook trout can be found in West Virginia's cool mountain streams. The trout are usually a green to dark brown color and can grow to be nearly 10 inches in length. The brook trout was also chosen by West Virginia fishermen as one of their favorite fish.

1 The Mountain State

West Virginia is located in the southeastern portion of the United States. With a total area of 24,230 square miles, it ranks forty-first in size among the fifty states. From north to south, West Virginia measures about 236 miles. From east to west it is close to 264 miles.

If you look at a map of West Virginia, you will see that its shape is unusual. To some, it almost looks like a frog with its two hind legs spread out. The "hind legs" are the two narrow strips of land called panhandles. The Northern Panhandle lies between Ohio and Pennsylvania, while the Eastern Panhandle cuts between Maryland and Virginia.

Much of West Virginia's land is mountainous. In fact, with an average elevation of 1,500 feet, West Virginia is the highest of any state east of the Mississippi River. For that reason, the state has been nicknamed the Mountain State. Some geographers believe that if West Virginia's mountainous

West Virginia's Borders

North: Pennsylvania and Maryland
South: Virginia
East: Virginia
West: Kentucky and Ohio

West Virginia's mountains are some of the oldest mountains in the world.

regions were flattened out, the area covered would extend well beyond the borders of the entire United States.

Mountains separate West Virginia's three main land regions. The Appalachian Ridge and Valley region is located east of the Allegheny Mountains. The Allegheny Mountains begin in central Pennsylvania and extend through West Virginia and Maryland. West Virginia's portion of the Alleghenies runs along the state's eastern border with Virginia. These are the tallest mountains in the state. West Virginia's highest point is located among these mountains. Spruce Knob rises more than 4,861 feet above sea level.

Spruce Knob, West Virginia's highest point, is located in the Monongahela National Forest.

The Appalachian Plateau region is located west of the Alleghenies. This region covers about 60 percent of West Virginia's total land area. It is also the state's most densely populated region. (This means that there are many people in each measured unit of land.) Among the major cities located there are Wheeling, Weirton, and Charleston, the state's capital.

The third West Virginia region includes the Blue Ridge Mountains. This range is located at the eastern tip of West Virginia's Eastern Panhandle. The mountains are part of the Appalachian Mountain chain that extends from Maine all the way down to Alabama. The Shenandoah Mountains are located in this region.

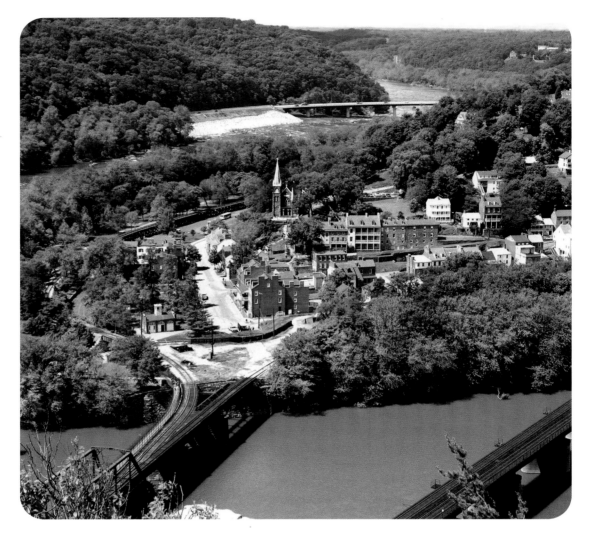

Harpers Ferry is located on the shores of the Potomac and Shenandoah rivers.

The Shenandoah River flows through West Virginia's Blue Ridge region. The river has deposited rich soil that supports the state's thriving peach and apple orchards. Martinsburg, the state's center of commerce and recreation, is located in this area. Another West Virginia river is the Potomac, which passes alongside Harpers Ferry—a scenic Blue Ridge town that played a major role in the country's history.

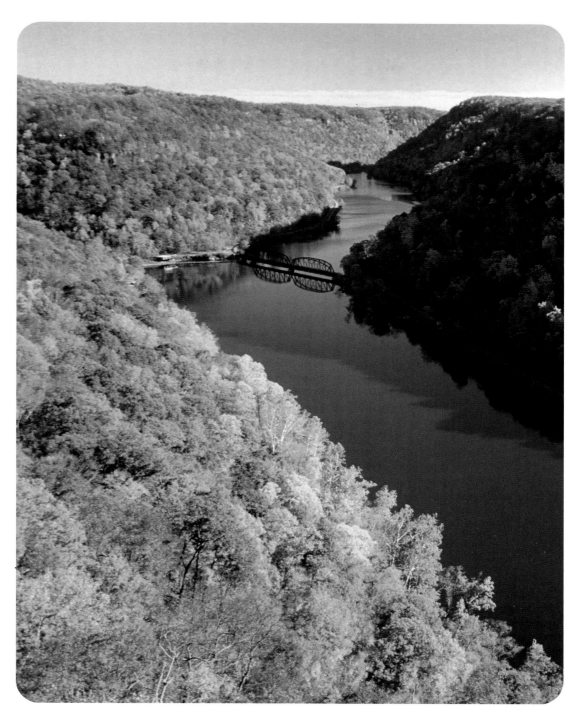

Autumn foliage covers the trees in the forests that border the New River Gorge.

Charleston, the state's capital, is located on the banks of the Kanawha River.

Waterways

Besides the Shenandoah and Potomac, there are other major rivers in the state. These include the Kanawha, Elk, Coal, Pocatalico, Little Kanawha, Guyandotte, Tug Fork, Big Sandy, Monongahela, Cheat, Tygart, West Fork, Back Creek, Cacapon, New, and Greenbrier rivers.

Rivers form several boundary lines between West Virginia and neighboring states. The Ohio River separates West Virginia from the state of Ohio. The Tug Fork and Big Sandy rivers define the state's borders with both Virginia and Kentucky. In the north, the Potomac River flows along West Virginia's border with Maryland.

Many of West Virginia's waterways lead to waterfalls.

West Virginia also has about seventy small lakes and ponds. All of them are man-made. Many of them were formed when dams were built across rivers and other waterways. These dams help control snowmelt, rainwater, and overflow from West Virginia's many rivers and streams. The state's largest reservoirs are Summersville Lake and Sutton Lake. Both are located in the central part of the state.

Climate

West Virginia has cold winters and hot summers. However, different regions in the state vary in average temperatures.

For example, residents living in the low-lying Appalachian Plateau may have summer temperatures around 87 degrees Fahrenheit. Temperatures in mountain towns, however, are a few degrees lower—about 82 degrees.

In January, the average low temperature in West Virginia's mountainous areas is 22 degrees. In the state's southernmost region, the average January low is 27 degrees. Even though the thermometers in West Virginia can hit below the freezing mark—below 32 degrees Fahrenheit—it is very unusual for winter temperatures to stay below freezing for more than a couple of days.

Storm clouds gather over the grassy fields of a farm. Heavy rains are common in parts of West Virginia during the year.

West Virginia's Eastern Panhandle, which is not too far from the Atlantic Ocean, experiences moderate coastal weather conditions throughout most of the year. Winds blowing in from the Atlantic Ocean help cool the heat in summer. These winds also keep the temperatures from getting too cold in the winter. West Virginia, however, occasionally experiences extreme weather conditions. The temperature soared to a sizzling 112 degrees Fahrenheit at Moorfield on August 4, 1930, and at Martinsburg on July 10, 1936. At the other extreme, the temperature fell to a bone-numbing -37 degrees Fahrenheit at Lewisburg on December 30, 1917.

West Virginia gets plenty of precipitation each year. Around 44 inches of water falls on the state as rain, sleet, or snow. Yearly snowfall varies throughout the state. It ranges from 20 inches in the southwest to nearly 100 inches in the mountainous areas. Very little snow falls in the coastal Eastern Panhandle area. At times, West Virginia can have too much precipitation. Flooding near the state's river valleys can be dangerous. In the past, overflowing rivers have destroyed entire West Virginia towns.

Wildlife

West Virginia is home to a variety of plants and animals. The forests in West Virginia are especially important to the state's wildlife. About three hundred years ago, the area that would become West Virginia was covered with thick forests. Over the years, however, forest fires and logging by humans reduced the number of trees in the region. Today, however, second-growth—trees that have grown after the original forest was cut

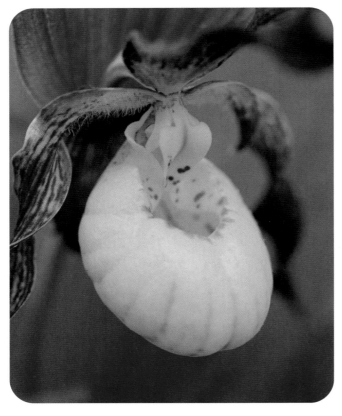

The yellow lady's slipper is one of the many plants found in West Virginia. The flowers of the lady's slipper plant often resemble shoes.

down—and later-growth trees are plentiful everywhere. In fact, they now cover about 80 percent of the state's total land area. Among these trees are softwoods such as spruce, hemlock, and white pine. Beech, hickory, sugar maple, and yellow birch, are found throughout the state. Hardwoods, such as cherry and oak, also thrive in West Virginia. All of these trees provide food or shelter for a number of the state's animals.

Trees are not the only plants that thrive in West Virginia. The Mountain State is also home to more than two hundred types of flowering plants and shrubs. These include the sawtooth sunflower, pitcher plants, bog rosemary, bloodroot, goldenrod, and azaleas.

Black bears, groundhogs, rabbits, raccoons, skunks, squirrels, bobcats, and white-tailed deer are just some of the animals that live on West Virginia land. A variety of birds nest in West Virginia's trees and fly through the state's skies. These include brown thrashers, cardinals, eagles, snipes, falcons, hawks, owls, quails, and scarlet tanagers. Different species of geese, ducks, and other water birds live on or alongside the state's waterways. The waters are also filled with many different types of fish, including walleye, bass, and trout.

The last century has brought great change to West Virginia's wildlife. As settlements grew, and towns and cities developed, a lot of wild land was used. Some species were forced to move to other regions of the state, or out of the state completely. Pollution caused by pesticides and other chemicals used by residents has also hurt West Virginia's wildlife. For example, toxic waste from the state's mines and steel mills seeped into some of the rivers. This poisoned most of the fish in those waterways. Not only did the fish population decline, but the animals that depended on the fish for food—such as eagles and hawks—no longer had a healthy food source.

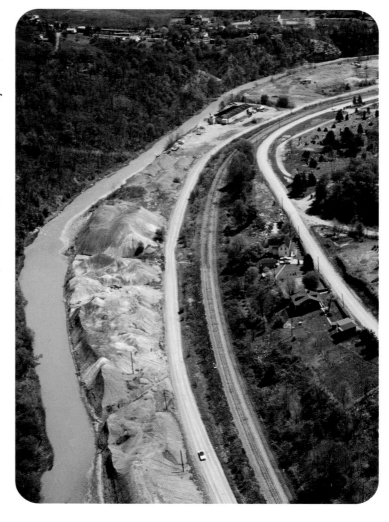

Waste from factories and mines has polluted many of West Virginia's waterways, such as Big Wheeling Creek.

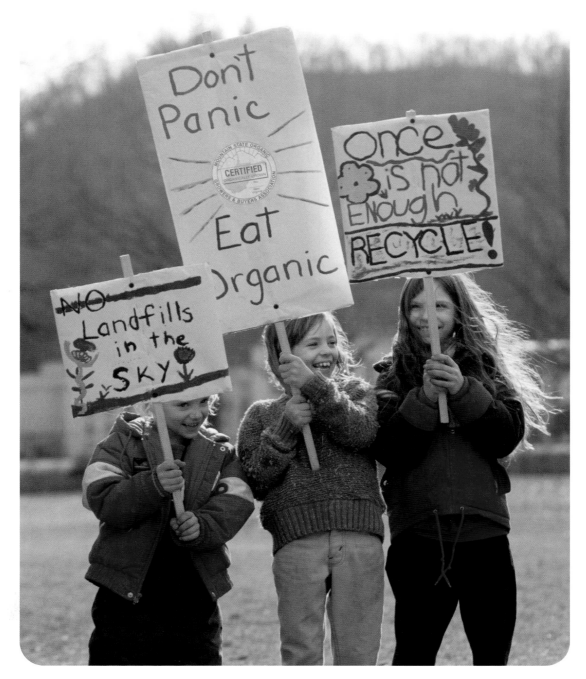

From pollution control to recycling programs, West Virginians of all ages have worked to protect their state's land and water.

A hiker pauses to admire the view from the Dolly Sods Wilderness Area.

Efforts have been made to clean up contaminated water and land. Tough laws and other regulations help to reduce factories' pollution. The hard work of dedicated residents and legislators has also resulted in protection for West Virginia wildlife. Wildlife sanctuaries and preserves help to protect native habitats. Laws have been passed that protect certain animals from hunting or any kind of human interference. Breeding programs and other conservation efforts have also helped some animal populations grow in the state. West Virginians treasure their land and work hard to preserve its natural beauty.

Plants & Animals

Sundew

Found in West Virginia's wetlands, such as bogs and marshes, the sundew is a type of carnivorous plant, which means that it eats meat. The sundew has sticky hairs, and when an insect lands on the hairs, it gets stuck and eventually dies. The sundew digests the insect's body, and uses those nutrients to survive and grow.

Mink

The mink is a member of the weasel family. A mink is dark brown and often has a white chin and a black-tipped tail. Like most weasels, the mink has a long, slender body and short legs. Mink live along rivers, streams, lakes, and ponds. Food for the mink includes frogs, mice, rats, fish, rabbits, crayfish, and small birds.

Red Fox

The West Virginia woods are home to the red fox. These small mammals are recognizable by their orange-red fur and bushy tails. The red fox eats fruits, berries, and grasses. But a fox will also eat other small animals, such as birds, squirrels, or mice.

Great Horned Owl

The great horned owl gets its name from its tufts of feathers on it head, which look like horns. This owl has a mixture of dark brown, white, and spotted feathers across its body. Its bright yellow eyes help it to hunt for prey, such as small rodents. Great horned owls can grow to be about 1 to 2 feet tall, with a wingspan of 3 to 5 feet.

Prickly Pear

The prickly pear is a type of cactus. Instead of having leaves like many other plants, the prickly pear has flat, fleshy pads that store water. Prickly pears can be found in West Virginia's steep rocky slopes and mountain foothills of the Appalachian Ridge and Valley and in the Blue Ridge Mountains. The oblong fruit of the prickly pear is a common food for a variety of West Virginia wildlife.

White-Tailed Deer

The white-tailed deer gets its name from the white coloring under its tail and on its rump. The coats of these graceful animals change with the season. In summer, their red-brown fur blends in with brown tree trunks. The fur becomes a grayish-brown during the gray winter months when tree trunks and grassy areas darken. Young white-tailed deer, called fawns, have reddish-brown fur peppered with white spots that eventually disappear. These spots help them hide among the grass and plants.

2 From the Beginning

North America's first residents were prehistoric people who came from Asia around 35,000 BCE They had traveled across a frozen land bridge that connected Asia—near present-day Siberia—to the land that is now Alaska. (The landbridge eventually disappeared into the ocean.) These people were the ancestors of Native Americans. As they traveled across the continent, they hunted animals such as caribou and deer, and gathered plants to eat, such as berries and other wild fruits.

Around 3000 BCE, these natives began to settle in the region that now includes West Virginia. Instead of moving from place to place in search of food, they began to form permanent settlements. The fertile soil was used to grow food, such as beans, corn, and squash. These early settlers also created large mounds. Historians believe that these mounds were important

The children of coal miners pose in front of their school in Rock Lick in 1920.

Today, the Grave Creek Mound is protected and only authorized experts are permitted to excavate or dig into the mound. In the past, however, many residents and visitors have dug beneath the mounds, destroying and removing historical artifacts that the Mound Builders buried.

for cultural activities like religious ceremonies. Their respected leaders were buried in these mounds, along with weapons and other valued items. Because of these mounds, some historians called these people the Mound Builders.

Mounds built by these cultures can be found throughout North and South America. One of the most famous burial mounds is the Grave Creek Mound in present-day Moundsville, West Virginia. This is a very wide mound that is nearly 70 feet tall. It is believed to be the largest cone-shaped burial site in North and South America.

By the end of the sixteenth century, the Mound Builders had disappeared, and no one knows exactly why. It is possible that many died from illness or lack of food. Or the mound-building people might have moved to other regions or joined other native groups.

At the start of the 1600s, several different native groups settled on the land that would eventually become West Virginia. These included the Cherokee, Shawnee, Delaware, Mingo, Seneca, Iroquois, Tuscarora, Ottawa, and Susquehannock, to name a few. Though they all traveled through the region to hunt for food, many of them also set up permanent settlements. For example, the Shawnee lived in small villages that were made up of round dwellings called wikkums, or wigwams. Besides hunting, the Shawnee also farmed. The Delaware also lived in small villages. These were usually near creeks, streams, and rivers. Their homes were called longhouses and were made of grass and bark.

New Arrivals

In the early 1600s, English colonists began arriving on North America's Atlantic coast. One of the areas the new colonists settled included present-day Virginia. In 1669, a German geographer named John Lederer was hired to explore the land west of the Virginia Colony. That land included present-day West Virginia. It is possible that Lederer was one of the first Europeans to set foot in the region.

Another British expedition, in 1671, traveled across the Appalachian Mountains. The explorers, Thomas Batts and Robert

The Sacred Bowl Game

Eastern Woodland Native Americans had a hunting range that included the area that is now West Virginia. Some of these native groups competed in the Sacred Bowl Game during winter ceremonies. They used a decorated wooden bowl and peach pits to play. Here is a version you can try.

What You Need

White Paper Plate

A shallow plastic bowl or container that can hold the paper plate

Black Marker

6 Almonds (pennies can be used if almonds are not available)

A bath towel

Divide a paper plate into 4 quarters with the black marker. Use the marker to draw one woodland animal or bird—a fox, eagle, bear, deer, beaver, wolf, for example—inside each quarter.

Place the paper plate inside the container.

If you are using almonds, blacken the top half of each of the six almonds with the marker.

Fold the bath towel into quarters and place it on the floor where you are going to play.

To Play the Game:

To play the game, assign each player an animal. Place the almonds or pennies on the plate in the container. Players take turns gently striking the container on the spot where the towel covers the floor. (You must do this gently and on the towel to keep the nuts or coins in the container, and to protect the container or the floor from damage.)

There are different ways to score the game:

A player scores a point and gets another turn if five of the six almonds turn up on the same (colored or uncolored) side. (If you use coins, you would count how many coins ended up heads or tails.) The winner is the person who first scores ten points.

You can also play the game by giving points based on how many almonds or coins land on the animal that the player chooses at the start of the game.

As explorers from Europe surveyed the region, they usually claimed the land for their countries.

Fallam, explored land near the New River that is now part of southern West Virginia. The area was claimed for Great Britain, and was called the Ohio Valley.

This newly discovered land had many fur-bearing animals, such as mink, beaver, and fox. The furs—or pelts—of these animals were often used to make clothing and other accessories for people in Europe and in other colonies. This fur trade encouraged more people to settle in the region.

British and French settlement in the area changed the lives of the Native Americans living there. Not only was some of their land taken away from these newcomers, but agreements and trading between Europeans and Native Americans affected the natives' way of life. Settlers traded guns, kettles, clothing, and other goods in exchange for furs the natives had collected. Many natives adopted the ways of life of the Europeans. In addition, many native groups used the guns and other European weapons against other native groups that did not have the same weaponry.

Further explorations and settlement continued. In the 1720s, settlers from Pennsylvania moved to the region that is now part of West Virginia's Eastern Panhandle. These settlers founded the town of Mecklenburg, which was later called Shepherdstown. Located on the banks of the Potamac River, it is the state's oldest European settlement.

As white settlers began moving into the region they took over the lands belonging to the Native Americans. As a result, fights often broke out between settlers and natives. To make matters worse, in 1754, the French and the British were fighting in

Settlers on horseback look to settle land around the hills of the region that would later be known as Moorfield.

the Ohio Valley. In Europe, both France and Great Britain had been warring with each other for decades. That conflict spilled over into North America and became known as the French and Indian War. It not only involved France and Great Britain, but also their Native American allies, who helped each side in the fight. Forts offered settlers protection from the fighting. Some settlements were actually located within the walls of the forts. For example, Fort Blair protected the city that is now known as Point Pleasant, and Fort Fincastle protected the village of Wheeling.

In 1763, the French and Indian War came to a close. Great Britain, the winner, gained all of France's land east of the Mississippi River. More settlers came to the region. The British attempted to maintain peace with the Native Americans by forbidding settlers from taking any land west of the Appalachian Mountains. Unfortunately, many settlers ignored this and continued to move westward.

A Mingo chief named Logan lived peacefully with the new white pioneers. However, in 1773 a group led by a man named Michael Cresap, killed many Shawnee and other Native Americans. In 1774, Cresap's men murdered many peaceful Mingo people, including members of Chief Logan's family. Angered by these attacks, Chief Logan joined forces with a Shawnee chief named Cornstalk to fight the settlers. Lord Dunmore, the British governor of the Virginia Colony, sent troops into western Virginia to fight Logan's and Cornstalk's warriors. The conflict became known as Lord Dunmore's War, and ended in 1774 when Dunmore's soldiers defeated the Native Americans at Point Pleasant. After this defeat, many Native American groups were forced to give up all their land claims south of the Ohio River.

In 1775, the colonist began fighting for their independence from the British. During the Revolutionary War, battles were fought throughout the different colonies. Many of the Native Americans in the Ohio Valley sided with the British. As colonists continued to settle Native American land that had been protected by British treaties, the natives continued to fight the colonists. The British encouraged this, because they hoped to weaken the revolutionary armies.

In 1777, colonial soldiers took Chief Cornstalk as a hostage. He had come in peace to warn a white settlement that the British were trying to convince Shawnees to attack white settlers. But the soldiers shot Chief Cornstalk in revenge for an attack by other Native Americans. Cornstalk's murder ended all peaceful relations between the Shawnee and the settlers in the region.

The American Revolution ended in 1783 with victory for the colonists. A short time afterward, settlers once again began pouring into the area that is now West Virginia. This settlement pushed remaining Native Americans farther west into present-day Indiana. A huge battle took place in 1794 at Fallen Timbers in present-day northwestern Ohio. Two thousand Native Americans, including Mingo, Shawnee, Delaware, Ottawa, Miami, and Chippewa warriors, fought against the new United States Army led by General Anthony Wayne. The Native Americans did not win, and eventually signed another treaty that gave up all their remaining claims to western Virginia.

The lives of pioneers living in western Virginia's mountainous regions were very different from the lives of the residents in eastern Virginia.

East and West

Residents of eastern and western Virginia did not agree on many things. Western Virginia was made up of frontier farming settlements. Eastern Virginia had bustling cities and large plantations. The plantation owners had a great deal of political power in the state. Residents in western Virginia did not feel they were well-represented in Virginia's government. To make matters worse, only men who were property owners could vote. Many farmers in West Virginia did not make enough money to own their own land, so they could not vote. Attempts were made to settle the differences between the regions. In 1850, all white men in Virginia were given the right to vote, even if they did not own property.

Slavery was another issue that divided the east from the west. Big plantations in the east depended upon slave labor to support their agricultural economy. Westerners did not need slaves to run their small farms, and many thought that slavery was wrong.

John Brown, who was a passionate abolitionist (a person who opposed slavery), and his followers made history when they raided the town of Harpers Ferry, in the hopes of starting a slave rebellion. United States forces fought back, and many of John Brown's men were killed—including Brown's son. Brown and the rest of his men were captured and tried in court for treason and murder. Brown was hanged in 1859, and six other raiders were also tried, found guilty, and executed. Though the raid on Harpers Ferry did not free accomplish what Brown had hoped, it did help other abolitionists' causes. Brown's actions brought more attention to the issue of slavery, angering people on both sides.

After the raid on Harpers Ferry, John Brown and his men tried to flee, but were captured, brought to trial, and found guilty.

A State is Born and Torn Apart

After the publicity that followed John Brown's failed raid, the slavery question grew in everyone's mind. Things began to really change in 1860 when Abraham Lincoln became president. He and his Republican Party were strongly against slavery. They wanted to prevent it from spreading into the new western territories. The southern slaveholders felt the decision on whether to be a free or slave state should be decided by each state, not by the federal government. The idea they supported became known as states' rights. The southern slaveholders were also concerned Lincoln would not only restrict slavery in any new western regions but would also rule against slavery in the southern states.

In 1861 South Carolina seceded from—or left—the Union. Then North Carolina, Georgia, Florida, Arkansas, and Tennessee, Alabama, Louisiana, Mississippi, and Texas, soon followed. The Civil War officially began in 1861. President Lincoln called for seventy-five thousand volunteers to fight in the war.

West Virginia had soldiers on both sides during the Civil War.

Virginia was still undecided about secession. Although the majority of western Virginian representatives wanted to stay a part of the Union, the state decided to secede on April 17, 1861. The state then joined the other ten southern states to form the Confederacy. Six months later, western Virginians decided they had had enough. They chose to break away from Virginia by a vote of 18,408 to 781. On June 20, 1863, President Lincoln signed a bill that admitted West Virginia as the nation's thirty-fifth state.

Unlike its neighbors to the east and south, West Virginia experienced few battles on its soil during the Civil War. A major one, however, did take place on November 6, 1863, at Droop Mountain. The Union Army easily defeated a large number of Confederate forces. All in all, more than 30,000 West Virginia men volunteered for the Union Army. But that does not mean that everyone in West Virginia supported with the Union. In fact, about seven thousand West Virginians fought on the side of the Confederacy.

A famous family feud between the Hatfields and the McCoys has its roots in the Civil War as well as in West Virginia history. The Hatfields of Logan County, West Virginia, sided with the Confederacy. The McCoys, from across the state line in Kentucky, sided with the Union. A bitter shooting war between the two families started when a pig from one family's farm ran away and was killed, cooked, and eaten by the other. Fighting between the two clans lasted several generations and resulted in a number of killings.

On February 3, 1865, West Virginia abolished slavery. Two months later, the Civil War finally came to an end when a treaty

was signed at the Appomattox Court House near Lynchburg, Virginia.

Industry

Between its admission into the Union and the early 1870s, agriculture was still an important part of West Virginia's economy. But industry became important, mostly because of improved technology and transportation.

Up until the early 1870s, West Virginia's many rivers served as the state's primary transportation routes. Rivers were the most efficient way for farmers and merchants to get their goods to market. After the Civil War, dams and locks were built on many of the rivers to help control the rivers' depths and flow. As a result, riverboat pilots could figure out easier and faster ways to haul goods such as produce, timber, clothing, and coal. The locks were

A steam engine arrives at a stop in Montgomery, West Virginia. The railroads made shipping goods easier, but they also brought tourists to the Mountain State.

designed to release huge quantities of stored water into shallow parts of the river when boats needed to pass through. This greatly increased river traffic and improved trade up and down West Virginia's many rivers. But even with improvements in riverboat transportation, there simply were not enough boats to keep up with West Virginia's booming timber and coal production. A perfect solution came in the form of railroad transportation.

In 1873, railroad workers completed the Chesapeake and Ohio Railroad in southern West Virginia. It connected the farmland community of Huntington to large cities on the Atlantic Coast. Other railroad lines were completed.

Coal Becomes King

The coming of the railroads, plus increased industrialization throughout the United States, increased the demand for coal. Coal was used to power the train engines and to keep factories running. Thanks to West Virginia's rich coal deposits, coal mining became the state's leading industry. By the late 1880s, the Mountain State's mines yielded more than one million tons of coal.

Many towns were founded near coal mines. The population grew as many immigrants from Europe came when they heard that coal mining in West Virginia was profitable. Unfortunately, what they had heard about and what they actually discovered to be true were two very different things.

Coal mining companies controlled everything. They managed the mines and owned all the equipment needed for mining. Miners had to pay the mining companies in order to use the tools and live in the housing near the mines. The fees

The mining companies owned all the housing that was close to the mines. Miners had no choice but to rent their homes from the mining companies.

were very high and were often taken out of the miners' pay. So the miners ended up making next to nothing for their hard work in the mines. Men and boys of all ages had to work in the mines to try to support their families.

Worst of all, the mines were unsafe and extremely dangerous to work in. On December 6, 1907, an explosion at a mine in Monongah killed 361 miners. By then, West Virginia's coal miners were at their breaking point. They could take not more. Something had to be done.

Labor Wars

Workers from factories, mills, mines, and other industries banded together in the 1880s to improve their lives. They wanted to fight the large controlling companies for better pay and safer working conditions. The groups that came together were called unions. The union created specifically for miners was called the United

Working in West Virginia's coal mines was a very dangerous and tiring job.

Mine Workers of America or UMWA. The UMWA had been able to successfully organize workers in Pennsylvania, Ohio, Indiana, and Illinois. However, unionization in West Virginia was very hard because the mine owners would not allow union people to recruit miners.

In 1912, miners at Paint Creek and Cabin Creek walked off the job, setting off a strike. A strike is when workers stop working in order to make a demand. Some of the things these miners wanted included the right to organize and better pay, safer working conditions, and a nine-hour workday.

The strike brought much violence to the state. Many miners and mine guards were killed. Many others were arrested and sent to prison. When Henry D. Hatfield became governor, he persuaded the mine owners to guarantee the miners a nine-hour workday and to let them organize a union.

During America's entry into World War I in 1917, the miners and mine owners cooperated with each other. West Virginia was able to provide a lot of coal to meet the country's fuel needs. By 1920, two years after World War I ended, the number of West Virginians who had joined the UMWA had grown to 50,000 workers. Around the same time, there was an increased demand for coal. So mine owners began opening new mines and improving mining methods.

In 1920, the UMWA attempted to organize miners in Logan and Mingo counties. However, the mine owners were determined to stop the unions in those two locations. To prevent unionization of the workers, mine owners drove workers from their company-owned homes. They were forced to live in tents to keep their jobs. During the winter of 1920 to 1921, violence once again broke out. Federal troops came in to maintain order.

However, violence continued into the early spring. On May 19, 1921, Governor E. F. Morgan proclaimed a state of war in Mingo County, which was known as Bloody Mingo. A few months later, about 3,000 miners from Paint Creek and Cabin Creek went to assist their Mingo County brothers. On August 31, 1921, a force of 1,200 state police and others faced a large group of angry miners outside of Logan. The fighting lasted for four days. Miners from Kentucky, Ohio, and northern West Virginia joined in to help the workers. The fighting grew so intense that President Warren G. Harding sent 2,100 federal troops and a group of United States Army bomber airplanes to restore order.

Realizing the hopelessness of fighting against the army, the miners finally surrendered. Their defeat discouraged further attempts at unionizing the workers. The miners also began to lose confidence in the union itself. As a result, West Virginia's membership in the UMWA dropped from 50,000 in 1920 to a few hundred in 1932. In 1933, things finally changed when federal laws recognized the importance of unions and protected them. West Virginia union organizers were once again back in action, only this time they were much more successful.

Depression, War, and Hope

While West Virginia was involved in violent labor conflicts, much of the rest of the United States was enjoying a period of economic success. The period became known as the Roaring 20s. Things came to a screeching halt, however, in 1929 when the stock market crashed. Many people lost their savings and could not pay for their homes. They stopped buying so many goods that many companies that made those goods collapsed. This great slowdown in economic activity eventually brought about the Great Depression.

The Depression hit West Virginia especially hard. Wages in the state were already lower than in other places. With factories producing fewer goods nationwide, less coal was needed. Many of West Virginia's miners lost their jobs. The Great Depression also affected farmers in the state. Many of them ended up losing their land because they could not afford to pay their taxes.

The Great Depression touched almost everyone in the United States. To help provide relief for the suffering country, President Franklin Delano Roosevelt created a set of programs that would help put people back to work and rebuild the country. One of his New Deal employment programs that was very successful in West Virginia was the Civilian Conservation Corps or CCC. This program gave West Virginia residents the

During the Great Depression, it was very hard for Americans to maintain their homes and farms. Farmsteads, like these in Randolph County, were often abandoned.

opportunity to work in the state's forests. Some of the jobs they accomplished included planting millions of trees, developing state and national parks, fighting forest fires, and creating hiking trails through West Virginia's wilderness. More than $7.5 million was spent on the CCC program in West Virginia. It provided housing for the young workers in the form of more than sixty camps that were set up throughout the state.

Another New Deal program that worked very well in West Virginia was the Federal Emergency Relief Administration or FERA. Under FERA, more than 60,000 West Virginians were put to work building roads and highways.

The United States' entered World War II after Japan's attack on Pearl Harbor on December 7, 1941. The war helped the nation's economy. Fuel, farm products, and other goods were needed for the military troops. Farms, factories, mills, and mines throughout the state were back in business.

The good times, unfortunately, did not last long. Once the war ended in 1945, West Virginia seemed to stumble while many other states enjoyed post-war prosperity. Coal production fell drastically as more people began to explore other forms of energy, such as gas, oil, and electricity. As a result, thousands of miners, once again, lost their jobs.

Disappointed with the constant changes from good times to bad times in the mining business, many people left West Virginia. They went off to search for better opportunities in other states. The state's population dropped in the 1950s and 1960s. Of those who stayed behind, many became unemployed. By the 1980s, West Virginia had the worst unemployment rate in the United States.

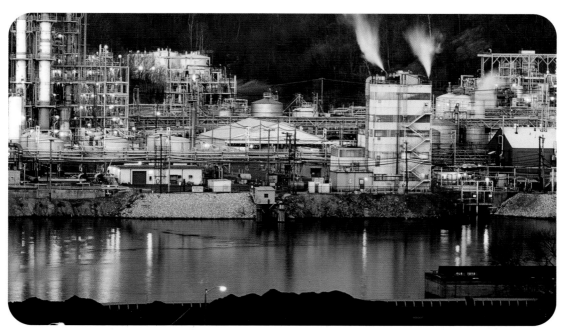

Though they have experienced tough times, West Virginia's factories and plants have provided jobs for state residents for many decades.

Remembering and honoring West Virginia's past has helped the state's present-day economy. Historical sites, such as the Heritage Farm Museum and Village in Huntington, help West Virginia's tourism industry.

Since the 1990s, however, West Virginia has made a comeback. The state government has worked hard to encourage the growth of new businesses and industries. For example, the state government has successfully persuaded computer software companies to move into the state. In addition, the state offered attractive conditions like low taxes to encourage the companies to build factories in many West Virginia cities.

Besides the increasing role of the state government in helping the economy, West Virginia's tourism business continues to grow every year. With the unspoiled natural beauty of the state's stunning forests, majestic mountains, and parks—plus the welcoming smiles of its many friendly residents—West Virginia is destined to receive more and more visitors in the years ahead. Indeed, its future looks very, very bright.

Important Dates

12,500 BCE (approximately) Paleo-Indians enter the region now known as West Virginia's Kanawha River Valley.

1000 BCE The Mound Builders live in the region.

1669 John Lederer, a German geographer hired by the governor of Virginia, explores what would become West Virginia.

1671 Explorers Thomas Batts and Robert Fallam reach the New River, which is in present-day southern West Virginia, and claim the surrounding area for England.

1727 German settlers from Pennsylvania move into what would become West Virginia's Eastern Panhandle. They establish West Virginia's oldest permanent settlement, now known as Shepherdstown.

Ann Maria Reeves Jarvis

1774 Chiefs Logan and Cornstalk are defeated by British forces at the Battle of Point Pleasant. Native American groups are forced to give up all land claims south of the Ohio River.

1859 Abolitionist John Brown leads a raid on Harpers Ferry.

1861 The Civil War begins. Virginia secedes from the Union, despite overwhelming opposition from representatives of western Virginia.

1863 West Virginia separates from Virginia and is admitted into the Union as the thirty-fifth state on June 20.

1873 The Chesapeake and Ohio Railroad is completed in southern West Virginia, connecting Huntington with large cities in the east.

1908 The first official service for Mother's Day is held in a church in Grafton. Inspired by West Virginia resident Ann Maria Reeves Jarvis, it is made an official holiday in 1914.

1921 Miners clash with 1,200 state police and 2,100 federal troops at Blair Mountain.

Flooding

1954 The West Virginia Turnpike is completed and opened for travel.

1985 A state lottery is established to raise money for the state.

1992 A law is passed to protect the state's groundwater.

2000 Shepherdstown hosts peace talks between Israel and Syria.

2002 President George W. Bush declares McDowell, Mingo, Wyoming, and Mercer counties disaster areas follow severe flooding.

3 The People

West Virginia's population is around 1,816,856. About 1,193,507 of these residents live in the state's rural areas. One of the reasons for the state's large rural population is due to the location of the coal mining industry in the remote mountains. Since the early 1880s, coal has been one of the major contributors to West Virginia's economy. Families whose members worked the coal mines settled in the mountainous areas close to the mines—away from the cities.

In West Virginia there are about seventy-five persons per seventy-five square miles. Most West Virginians live along the banks of the Kanahwa, Monongahela, and Ohio Rivers.

West Virginia cities are on the small side. The four largest cities in West Virginia are Charleston, Huntington, Parkersburg, and Wheeling.

Many towns and cities throughout the state are nestled among West Virginia's hills and mountains.

Charleston, the state's capital and largest industrial center, has a population of approximately 51,394. This port city is conveniently located at the junction of the Kanahwa and Elk Rivers. Huntington has a population of about 49,533. Another small port city, Huntington is on the Ohio River near the mouth of the Big Sandy River. Huntington has become the Mountain State's main center of trade and transportation.

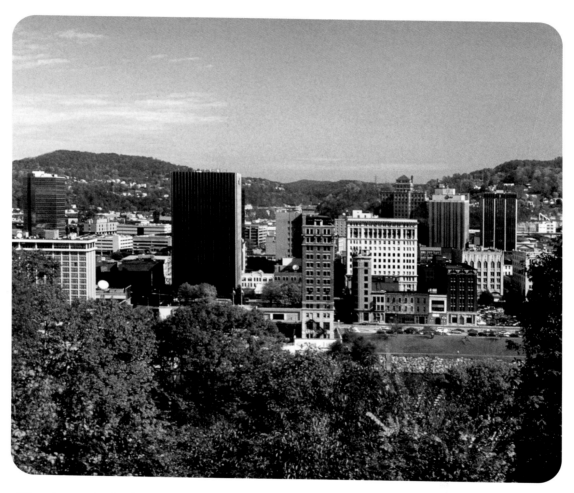

Charleston is the home of the state government and many profitable industries.

Lewisberg residents enjoy a food tasting festival. West Virginia has many thriving cities and towns.

Parkersburg is located on the Ohio River at the mouth of the Little Kanahwa River. It was founded during West Virginia's late nineteenth-century oil boom. Since then it has grown into a major manufacturing center where many goods are produced. The city has a population of about 32,000. The Northern Panhandle city of Wheeling is the Mountain State's center of iron and steel manufacturing. It has a population of a little more than 30,000. Other major cities are the manufacturing and shipping centers of Morgantown, Fairmont, and Clarksburg.

Famous West Virginians

Daniel Boone: Explorer and Scout

Daniel Boone, who was born in 1734, was the first English-speaking American to scout what was known as the Appalachian West. He surveyed and cut a trail from Virginia through the Cumberland Mountains into Kentucky. The trail, which was called the Wilderness Trail, became the main route into Tennessee. Boone also lived at Clendenin's Settlement, known today as Charleston, West Virginia.

Mary Lou Retton: Olympic Gymnast

During the 1984 Summer Olympics, sixteen-year-old Mary Lou Retton from Fairmont, West Virginia, became the center of media and public attention. She won the gold medal for all-around gymnastic perform-ance. She was the first American to win a gold medal in the international competition in thirty-six years.

Booker T. Washington: Educator and Reformer

Born on 1856, Booker T. Washington grew up in Malden, West Virginia, where he worked in the area's coal mines and salt furnaces. He loved to read and learn, and eventually earned a college degree and moved to Alabama. While living there, he founded the Tuskegee Institute, a college dedicated to serving black youth. In addition, he founded the National Negro Business League. He promoted greater cooperation between African Americans and white people. He also wrote a best-selling autobiography, Up from Slavery, *which was published in 1901.*

Pearl S. Buck: Author

The daughter of missionary parents working in China, Pearl S. Buck was born in Hillsboro, West Virginia, in 1892. As a youngster, Buck had a passion for writing and began submitting stories to local newspapers. In her late thirties, she wrote a novel about a Chinese family entitled The Good Earth. *It won the Pulitzer Prize in fiction in 1932. In 1938, Buck became the first American woman to win the Nobel Prize in literature. Her other best-selling books include* East Wind, West Wind; Dragon Seed; *and* The Living Reed.

Chuck Yeager: Aviation Pioneer

Chuck Yeager, who was born in Myra in 1923, was a World War II fighter pilot who became a test pilot after the war. In 1947, he made history by becoming the first pilot to fly faster than the speed of sound. Writer Tom Wolfe wrote about Yeager and the United States' first astronauts in his book The Right Stuff, *which later became a highly praised movie. Today, Charleston's airport is named in Chuck Yeager's honor.*

Thomas "Stonewall" Jackson: Confederate General

A brilliant military planner, Thomas "Stonewall" Jackson, born in Clarksburg on January 21, 1824, was one of the greatest generals of the Confederacy during the Civil War. His forces defeated the Union Army at the First Battle of Bull Run, where he earned his nickname. The odds were not in Jackson's favor, but he and his men stood strong "like a stone wall." Jackson's last battle was fought at Chancellorsville, where he was accidentally wounded by his own troops. He died a few days later.

Many events across the state—such as this Italian heritage festival—honor the ethnic heritage of West Virginia's diverse residents.

West Virginians

About 95 percent of West Virginians are white. Many of these residents are descendants of European settlers who came to the area hundreds of years ago. Others are related to colonial settlers who came from Virginia, Pennsylvania, New York, New Jersey, Delaware, and Maryland. Around the same time, Pennsylvania settlers of Scotch-Irish and German descent also made their way into the region.

At the turn of the twentieth century, immigrants from Ireland, Italy, Poland, and Hungary also arrived in the state seeking work in the growing coal, lumber, and manufacturing industries. Some of the descendants of these later arrivals can still be found today in West Virginia's coal-mining regions and industrial centers. Their rich culture and traditions are very much alive, too. Examples include Lewis County's Irish Spring Festival and Clarksburg's Italian Heritage Festival.

African Americans make up about 3 percent of West Virginia's population. Some of these West Virginians have ancestors who entered the state between 1870 and 1930. They came from Kentucky, Pennsylvania, and Tennessee to work in the Mountain State's coal mines. A small percentage of West Virginia's African Americans are also descendants of slaves who once worked in the region's salt and coal mines before the Civil War.

The mining boom drew many African Americans families to the state. Some of their descendants still live in West Virginia.

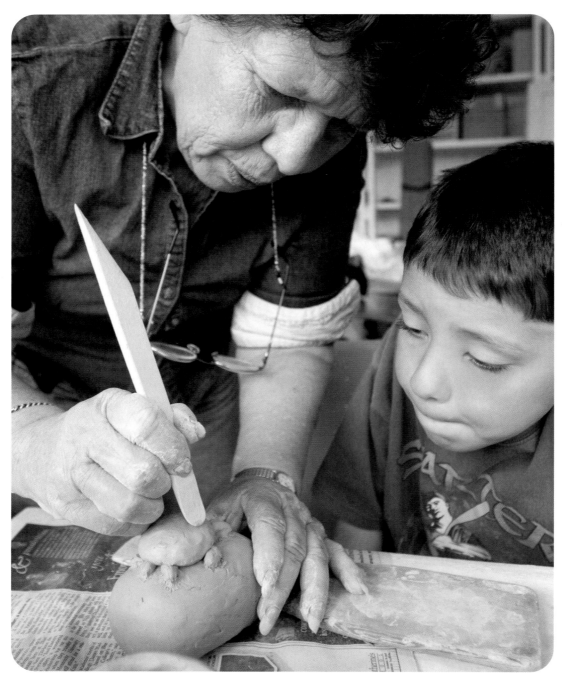

Native American cultural centers in West Virginia keep native traditions alive through programs—like this art class—that teach younger generations about their heritage.

People of Hispanic or Latino heritage make up less than 1 percent of the state's population. Asians and Asian Americans represent only a little more than half a percent of the population. Native Americans, who once were the only people living in the region, make up an even smaller portion of the population—only .2 percent. Despite these low numbers, all of these West Virginians—no matter what their background may be—play important roles in the state. Besides sharing their heritage and culture—through events around the state—all West Virginia residents play an important role in the state's economy. It is this mixture of history, culture, and industry that helps to make the Mountain State strong.

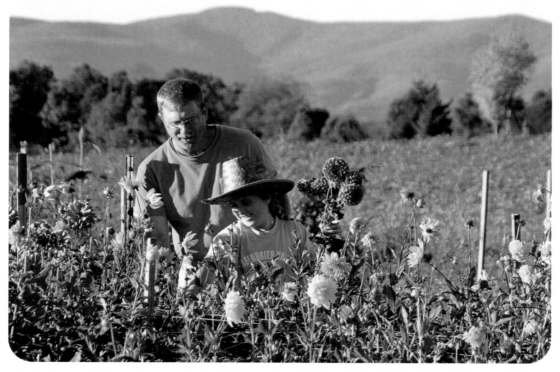

A father and daughter work in their garden in Frankford. West Virginians of all ages and backgrounds take pride in their state and are proud to be residents of the Mountain State.

Calendar of Events

Gardner Winter Music Festival

Visitors can get a strong sense of West Virginia's musical heritage at the Gardner Winter Music Festival, held in late February. The festival showcases traditional Appalachian music performed by musicians from West Virginia, Kentucky, Virginia, Pennsylvania, Ohio, and other states.

Irish Spring Festival

A town in Lewis County, West Virginia, called Ireland, was founded by an Irishman named Andrew Wilson. He lived to be 114 years old. To honor his long life span, as well as the town's Irish heritage, the town holds a weeklong celebration. Events include a pot o'luck dinner, costume contests, square dancing, a scavenger hunt, a "lucky charm" horseshoe pitch, a fried potato contest, and plenty of Irish music.

Blue and Gray Reunion

One of the first battles of the Civil War was fought over Barbour County's Philippi Bridge, which is West Virginia's longest and oldest covered bridge. The 143-foot bridge, built in 1852, is still standing. Every June a reenactment of the historical fight takes place there.

Cherry River Festival

This weeklong festival in Richwood celebrates the city's coal mining history. Events include a fishing contest, outdoor concerts, pageants, a pet show, fireworks, a dance, a truck and car show, and more.

A town festival

Italian Heritage Festival

Every Labor Day weekend, Clarksburg pays tribute to West Virginia's Italian Americans with this fun-filled event, which attracts over 100,000 visitors each year. The event features authentic Italian food, top-name entertainers, and games for people of all ages.

Leaf Peepers Festival

This event in Tucker County is held in late September. That is when West Virginia's forests are ablaze with bright autumn colors of orange, red, and yellow. Besides leaf peeping, visitors can check out the area's food and craft fair and the family dog show.

Charleston Sternwheel Regatta

West Virginia's capital hosts this Labor Day weekend event. It celebrates the Kanawha River's history and the charm of the sternwheeler boats that have paddled along its banks for close to two hundred years. In addition to seeing the boats, visitors can attend free concerts, watch the regatta's Grand Feature Parade, or view a spectacular fireworks display in the evening.

West Virginia Black Walnut Festival

When a West Virginian named Henry Young sold two million pounds of the region's black walnuts in 1954, the residents of Spencer thought it was a good reason to celebrate. The festival has grown to become a four-day, mid-October event that includes a parade, exhibits, live music, arts and crafts, and other fun-filled activities.

The Charleston Sternwheel Regatta

4 How It Works

As in all states, there are different levels of government in West Virginia. The towns and cities have their own local government. Many cities and towns in the Mountain State are led by a mayor or manager and council members. These local governments often handle issues such as zoning or land use.

West Virginia's towns and cities are grouped together—based on their location—to form counties. West Virginia is divided into fifty-five counties. Each county is managed by a county commission. Each county commission is made up of three county commissioners who are elected to serve six-year terms. The commissioners oversee such things as maintaining parks and roads, as well as providing local police protection and library services. Other officials elected within each county include the sheriff, as well as the chief law enforcement officer, prosecuting attorney, tax assessor, circuit clerk, county clerk, and land surveyor. All are elected to serve four-year terms.

On a statewide level, West Virginia is headed by a governor who is elected to a four-year term. The Mountain State also has

The Capitol in Charleston.

thirty-four state senators and one hundred delegates. Each senator or delegate represents specific regions or districts in the state. The state also has representatives at the national level. Eligible voters

Branches of Government

Executive West Virginia's executive branch is charged with making sure that the state's laws are carried out. A governor, who is elected to a four-year term, heads up the executive branch. The governor has the power to veto, or to reject, laws or parts of laws that the state legislature passes. As chief executive of the state, he or she also has the power to prepare a budget, choose department heads, call out the National Guard during emergencies, and other powers. The executive branch also includes the secretary of state, the auditor who supervises the state's finances and budget, and the state attorney general. Like the governor, each is elected to a four-year term.

Legislative West Virginia's legislative branch is in charge of making and amending (or changing) the state's laws. The legislature is divided into two houses: the Senate and the House of Delegates. The Senate has thirty-four members, or senators, who are elected to four-year terms. The House of Delegates has one hundred members who are elected to two-year terms. When both houses agree on a bill, it is sent to the governor for his or her signature. Once the governor signs the bill, it becomes law.

Judicial The judicial branch of West Virginia's state government is responsible for interpreting the laws that the state's legislature passes. West Virginia's highest court is the State Supreme Court of Appeals, which rules on whether laws are in agreement with West Virginia's constitution. The judicial branch also includes circuit, magistrate, and municipal courts.

elect two senators to serve six-year terms in Washington, D.C., and three members of the House of Representatives to serve two-year terms.

From Bill to Law

West Virginia's elected representatives often write and propose bills in response to the concerns of ordinary citizens. The process follows five principal stages: committee action, floor action, action by the second committee, conference committee action, and action by the governor.

In 1928, Minnie Buckingham Harper became the first African-American woman to serve in a state legislature. She served in West Virginia's House of Delegates, in her husband's position after he passed away.

Before a delegate introduces a bill, the clerk of the senate or house identifies the bill with a number. That number is used to refer to the bill throughout the period of consideration. Once the bill is numbered, the president of the senate or the speaker of the house gives the bill to a standing committee. A standing committee is a small group of senators or delegates who are assigned to study bills about specific subjects. For example, a senate standing committee might be made up of senators who are experts in crime control. This process enables more bills to be studied because they go directly to those who are experts in their field.

After the standing committee examines the bill, the committee files a written report. The report will state whether the committee recommends passing the bill—perhaps with amendments, or additions—or rejecting it. Some bills "die in committee." That means the committee members may not have had the time needed to study the bill or that the members may have decided the bill should not be

West Virginia's legislators discuss, approve, and reject laws in the State Capitol.

recommended to the other members of the senate or house for action.

If the committee recommends passing the bill, it is then reported to the members of the house or the senate, where it is read three times. During the first reading, the members of the house or senate are simply told that a bill is about to be considered. On the second reading, members vote on the amendments suggested by the committee, as well as the amendments individual members of the house or senate may have proposed. Voting on the passage of the bill takes place during the third reading. If a bill passes in one house, it is sent to the other and the process is repeated.

If the second house makes changes to a bill, it is sent back to the other house to see if its members agree. If they do not agree and the second house refuses to remove the changes, a conference committee is called. The conference committee is made up of an equal number of members from each house. Their job is to try to work things out.

If the conference committee reaches a compromise, both houses must adopt its ruling and vote on the bill again. After a bill passes both houses, it is sent to the governor, who either signs the bill into law or vetoes it. If the governor vetoes the bill, the legislature may vote to override the veto. If the legislature then reaches a majority vote in favor of passing the bill, it can override the governor's veto. When that happens, the bill becomes law without the governor's approval.

You Can Make A Difference

Many ideas for laws come from everyday ordinary citizens. It is the job of the state legislators to listen to the residents' concerns and ideas. If you have in issue that you think is important to your state, do not be afraid to talk about it. You can ask your parents, teachers, or media specialists to help you research the issue and how to bring it to the attention of your state legislators. You can make a difference.

To find your state legislators, visit
this Web site:
http://www.legis.state.wv.us/
You will need to know the name of the voting district in which you live. If you are not sure, ask a parent, teacher, or media specialist to help you.

5 Making a Living

For a state marked with so many resources and much natural beauty, West Virginia has had its share of economic ups and downs. Its once-flourishing coal mining and steel manufacturing industries have suffered downturns as the nation's economy changed. Coal production dropped dramatically after World War II when industries switched to other sources of energy such as gas and oil. As a result, thousands of miners lost their jobs.

Steelworkers were faced with the same problem when demand for steel was drastically reduced. Foreign countries outside of the United States began to offer their steel at cheaper prices throughout the 1980s and into the early 1990s. Coupled with the loss of jobs, many unemployed workers began leaving the state.

Today, West Virginia's mining, manufacturing, and service industries seem to be in better shape. Demand for coal is up. However, to make sure that the state's economy stays healthy, it has become necessary for state governmental officials to attract newer businesses to the state. Thanks to their efforts, numerous

Though the industry has had its ups and downs, mining in West Virginia still remains an important part of the state's economy.

Several laboratories and other research facilities are based in the state. These businesses rely on the skills of many hardworking West Virginians.

computer software companies have moved into an area between Morgantown and Clarksburg. This had led some Mountain State residents to call that region Software Valley.

Many federal government operations have moved from Washington, D.C., to West Virginia. As a result, the Fingerprint Center of the FBI (the Federal Bureau of Investigation, which employs agents who investigate federal crimes) is now a major employer in Clarksburg. In addition, the Computing Center of the Internal Revenue Service or IRS—the government agency that collects income taxes—has opened in Martinsburg.

The agricultural industry in West Virginia does not represent a large part of the state's economy. But there are still many farms located throughout the state. Some of these farms have been in business for several decades.

Agriculture

West Virginia has very little flat land, so it is very difficult to grow crops there. So agriculture only represents a very small percentage of the state's economy. Despite this, farms cover more than 3 million acres of West Virginia land. That is about one-quarter of the state's total land area. Many of these farms are livestock farms or ranches. They raise cattle for meat and dairy products, sheep, turkeys, and chickens.

Among West Virginia's major cash crops are tobacco, corn, and hay. The Eastern Panhandle region is also well known for its peach and apple orchards. In fact, the Golden Delicious apple was first introduced in the United States by farmers from West Virginia's Eastern Panhandle.

Recipe for Blackberry Crumble

Blackberries have long been a favorite among West Virginians since the early days of settlements. Wild blackberries were often picked to make tasty dishes. Later, many residents grew blackberries in their own gardens and yards. Follow this easy recipe to make a tasty blackberry dessert.

Ingredients:

2 cups blackberries—either fresh, frozen, from a can or a jar

2/3 cup sugar

2 tablespoons butter or margarine

3/4 cup all-purpose flour

1/8 teaspoon salt

Have an adult preheat the oven to 350 degrees Fahrenheit. While the oven is heating, you can put together the ingredients. If the blackberries are fresh, have an adult help you wash them.

In a mixing bowl, combine the sugar and blackberries. Pour this mixture into a baking dish.

In a separate bowl mush the butter or margarine until it is almost creamy. Mix in the flour and salt. Sprinkle this mixture over the blackberries in your baking pan.

Bake the dessert for about 35 to 40 minutes at 350 degrees. When it is done, the crumbly top should be a golden brown.

Have an adult help you take the dessert out of the oven—the dish will be hot! Let the blackberry crumble cool a little bit before serving it. The warm crumble can be served plain or with a scoop of your favorite ice cream.

Industry

Industry, including mining and manufacturing, makes up about a third of the state's economic profits. The Mountain State's most valuable mineral resource is still coal. West Virginia is the nation's third-leading coal-producing state, just behind Wyoming and Kentucky.

What makes West Virginia's coal very valuable is that it causes very little pollution when it is burned. As technology has improved, mining companies have found more efficient ways to mine coal. Unfortunately, in some ways, this improved machinery has made life hard for miners in the state. While the new equipment helps them mine more coal at a faster rate, it also results in the need for fewer miners. So many mining jobs are lost. As a result, some of West Virginia's richest coal-mining regions, particularly those in the southern portion of the state, have been hit with high rates of unemployment. The miners are not the only

Much of West Virginia's coal is transported by large barges that travel up and down the state's rivers.

ones who lose their jobs. People who live and work around the mining communities also suffer when there are fewer people living—and spending money—near the mines.

West Virginia has other valuable natural resources. Natural gas, which is used for energy, is mined in the state. Limestone can be found in West Virginia's rocks. The limestone is collected and used for construction in the state and around the country. Sand and gravel found in the state—much of it taken from the bottom of the Ohio River—are also used in construction. The state's many forests provide wood for the lumber industry. This wood is used to make furniture, construction material, baseball bats, and other useful goods.

Manufacturing is an important West Virginia industry. Factories in the state make many chemical products. These include paints, plastics, detergents, and dyes. The state's many steel mills also contribute to the manufacturing industry.

Services

More than 60 percent of the money West Virginia makes from its economy comes from the state's service industry. The service industry includes any jobs that provide a service for people instead of making a product that can be sold. Examples of service industry workers include teachers, salesclerks, librarians, insurance agents, doctors, real estate agents, bankers, and tour guides. More than half of the jobs in West Virginia are service jobs.

The most important service industry in the Mountain State is tourism. Bringing in more than 3 million dollars each year, tourism has already outperformed coal mining as the state's largest industry. West Virginia has plenty to offer, especially for those who love outdoor activities. During the winter months, the state's breathtaking mountains attract many skiers every year. White-water rafting is another popular sport, and West Virginia's many fast-flowing rivers give visitors a lot of opportunities. There are also plenty of activities for those who enjoy hiking, camping, boating, fishing, and rock climbing. People who come to do these fun outdoor activities spend money in the state for food, lodging, souvenirs, and sporting equipment.

Visitors are also drawn to the state's many indoor activities. A popular destination is the John Brown Wax Museum in Harpers Ferry. Visitors go to the museum to learn about John Brown's attempt to start a slave rebellion and end slavery. Another popular tourist site is the Parkersburg Oil and Gas Museum. The exhibits there feature engines, equipment, and tools used in the early days of the state's oil and gas industry. West Virginia has other histori-cal sites that attract many people every year. From colonial sites to pioneer villages to Native American culture centers, visitors can come to the state and learn about West Virginia's history.

West Virginia's many restaurants, hotels, and entertainment sites are also

West Virginia's many mountains and cliffs draw many experienced rock climbers to the state.

Products & Resources

Coal

Coal has long been identified with West Virginia. In the late 1890s, most people came to the state to work in the coal mines. Though some of the state's mines are no longer in use, many other mines still employ Mountaineers who work in this important industry. Every year, West Virginia's mines produce more than 100 metric tons of coal.

Natural Gas

Natural gas is mined and used for energy—for example, to heat homes or provide power for industries. Natural gas is West Virginia's second most important natural resource. It is found in the hills in the central and west central regions of the state, and in the upper Ohio and Little Kanawha valleys.

Salt

Salt mining was West Virginia's first important industry. The state's salt deposits are found deep underground, with the richest mines located in Marshall County. West Virginia salt is shipped throughout the country—and the world—to be used to season food or as an ingredient in other products.

Limestone

Millions of years ago, the region that included West Virginia was covered by seas and lakes. Many minerals, such as calcite, collected at the bottom of these bodies of water. When these seas and lakes dried up over time, the rocks that held these minerals were exposed. Limestone comes from rocks that are made from calcite. The limestone is collected and used to build roads and other concrete structures. Most of the state's limestone can be found in eastern West Virginia.

Golden Delicious Apples

West Virginia farmers introduced the Golden Delicious apple in the United States. It has lightly freckled bright yellow skin on the outside. The inside of this crisp apple is sweet and juicy. The Golden Delicious apple is perfect for cooking, especially in making applesauce and apple juice. This apple became West Virginia's state fruit in 1995.

Glassware

Glass comes from certain crystals and other materials that are heated at very high temperatures. When it is hot enough, this mixture turns into a thick liquid. Glass objects—called glassware—are made when skilled workers shape the liquid into shapes and designs. West Virginia glassmakers are known for the attractive designs of their figurines, sculptures, cups, and stained glass windows.

73

West Virginia's many museums and historical sites honor the state's past, while playing an important role in West Virginia's tourism industry.

an important part of the service industry. Residents and visitors spend money to dine, shop, and enjoy other fun activities in the state's busy cities and towns. Besides earning money for the economy, all of these tourism activities provide jobs for many West Virginians.

Thanks to the efforts of all of West Virginia's hard-working people, the state has remained one of the most frequently visited and best-loved states in the nation. It is West Virginians' spirit of dedication, passion, ingenuity, and old-fashioned friendliness that will create a very bright future for the Mountain State in the years ahead.

West Virginia's state flag, which was adopted in 1929, features the state seal against a white field bordered in blue.

The state seal displays a farmer and a miner. Between them is a large rock draped in ivy. The rock contains the date of West Virginia's admission to the Union. In front of the farmer and miner are two rifles. Resting on top of them is a cap of liberty. Above the farmer and miner is a red banner with the words "State of West Virginia" written in black. A horseshoe-like arrangement of rhododendrons—the state flower—surrounds the rest of the seal

Chester

Weirton

Wheeling

70

Moundsville

Grave Creek Mound
State Historic Site

Coopers Rock
State Forest

250

Morgantown

68

Fairmont

Kingwood

Keyser

250

Ohio R.

Parkersburg

Harrisville

50

Clarksburg

50

Monongahela
National Forest

Smoke Hole
Caverns

522

Martinsburg

81

220

50

79

Buckhannon

250

219

Petersburg

S. Br. Potomac R.

BLUE

Harper
National Histori

Little Kanawha R.

77

Point Pleasant

Ravenswood

Ripley

33

119

33

Elkins

33

Seneca
Caverns

Spruce Knob

220

33

APPALACHIAN MOUNTAINS

SHENANDOAH MT.

CHEAT MOUNTAIN

35

Elk R.

79

Sutton

19

250

219

National Radio
Astromony Observatory

Seneca
State Forest

64

Huntington

Charleston

Gauley River National
Recreation Area

Summersville

Madison

60

Carnifex Ferry
Battlefield
State Park

NEW MOUNTAINS

Monongahela
National Forest

ALLEGHENY MOUNTAINS

Chief Logan
State Park

119

77

19

60

Greenbrier R.

Gyandotte R.

Exhibition
Coal Mine

New R.

Lost World
Caverns

Lewisburg

Organ Cave

64

Beckley

Tug Fork R.

52

77

Panther
State Forest

ALLEGHENY MOUNTAINS

219

Bluefield

	Interstate		State Capital		National Forest
	Major Highway		Highest Point in State		State Forest
	Appalachian Trail		Mountains		State Park
	City or Town		Historic Site		Other Points of Intere

0   miles   50

76

The West Virginia Hills

Words by Ellen King
Music by H. E. Engle

mf

Oh, the West Vir-gin - ia hills! How ma - jes - tic and how grand, With their

sum-mits bathed in glo - ry, Like our Prince Im-man-uel's Land! Is it an - y won-der then, That my

heart with rap - ture thrills As I stand once more with loved ones On those West Vir-gin - ia hills?

CHORUS

Oh, ___ the hills, beau - ti - ful hills, How I

love those West Vir-gin - ia hills! If o'er sea o'er land I roam, Still I'll

think of hap - py home, And my friends a-mong the West Vir-gin - ia hills.

State Song

77

More About West Virginia

Books

Heinrichs, Ann. *West Virginia*. Minneapolis, MN: Compass Point Books, 2004.

Hodgkins, Fran. *West Virginia*. Mankato, MN: Capstone Press, 2004.

Naylor, Phyllis Reynolds. *Shiloh*. New York: Atheneum, 1991.

Web Sites

Official West Virginia State Web Portal
http://www.wv.gov

West Virginia Kids' Page
http://www.legis.state.wv.us/Educational/Kids_Page/kids.htm

Wild & Wonderful—West Virginia Tourism
http://www.westvirginia.com

About the Author

Rick Petreycik has written several books for young readers. He has also written articles on history, music, film, travel, health, safety, and business for *American Legacy, Rolling Stone, Yankee, Disney Magazine, The Oxford American, Profit, Performing Songwriter, Safety + Health,* and *The Hartford Courant.* He lives in Connecticut with his wife and daughter.

Index

Page numbers in **boldface** are illustrations.